HESITATIONS

POEMS BY

WAYNE LANTER

Twiss Hill Press
Freeburg, Illinois

Also by Wayne Lanter

Poetry
The Waiting Room
Threshing Time
At Float on the Ohta-gawa
Canonical Hours
A Season of Long Taters
In This House of Men

Poetry Anthology
New Century North American Poets

Chapbooks
Gothic Coffee House
Threlkeld
Wyandotte
Running on Grass
The Anniversary
Leaving the Cloister
Spoken Word Sundays
Conversations with a Barn
Corn Husking Vacation
At the River's Edge
Poems from the Midwest I
Poems from the Midwest II
Poems from the Midwest III
The Second Coming
The Stone in the Road
Until We Meet Again
A Foot of Snow – A Little Bit of Sunshine
Final Coins of Fortune
Snakezy

Fiction
The Final Days
Psyaint David

Non-fiction
Defending the Citadel
If the Sun Should Ask

HESITATIONS

Twiss Hill Press
P. O. Box 122
Freeburg, Illinois

ISBN-10:09838412-4-1
ISBN-13:978-0-9838412-4-1
LCCN-2016910691

To Bobbi, Nathan & Joshua,
for their kindness, affection and love.

If this world is a poem, it is not because we see
the meaning of it at first but on the strength of
its chance occurrences and paradoxes.
— Maurice Merleau-Ponty

CONTENTS

Wayne Lanter

What We Say Here

The world still remembers though
it might have lost or misplaced
the scorecard that recorded the names
that fabled day with the game on the line
the ninth inning version of American
Baseball roulette of pitch and toss
of the outfielders Satch called in
to sit on the grass and who sat immobile
less than ninety-feet from the plate
trusting Satch or chance or probability
to throttle-down or hold in check
the better parts of Josh Gibson's power
who assented to the comic arrogance
of Casey's grapefruit splattered
on Gabby's head or of Gehrig and Reiser
taking on iron fences and concrete walls
the players penciled into the outfield
that inning persuaded to drop their gloves
and sit cross-legged
a short lethal distance from the plate
to watch Satch taunt and bait Gibson
with a variety of now you see it now
you don't pitches
and then with a flourish of fast-balls
to strike him out

1

Awakening

Beneath the blue-hue of TV light,
as violet as the blanket someone dropped
on his wet fur, the dog lies motionless,
humped up and undefined, breathing softly,
ruminating in his womb, waiting a caress,
a sign that says, "Here's the plan, the next act,
scene one about to begin," prepared to rise
and walk in whatever direction survival asks.

This is the essence of form, a pillow-fabric
sack of shaved wool from some ram's back.
Or better yet, a modern artifact designed
simply to rise and walk toward sunlight.

   Prodded from our interior, we seek light.
   Called from our darkness we rue the night.

Yassar Arafat
Returns to al Sahar

Today a Simoom clouds the Negev sun.
al-Turi woman stir tent fires and listen.
The cries of a dying child, an old man's voice.
Goats move like ghosts among tent-fires.
al-Turi women tend their sand-water wells.
They watch the sky.
Arafat's plane is down, the shaman lost, presumed dead.
They expected this, the blood rain, a sea of darkness.
They nod and knead unleavened bread.
By midnight, tent fires dim to a glow.
Beneath the night sky they listen to old men grumbling.
The cries of a dying child rise from the embers.
The message today is severe, the omen prescient.
A broken fuselage lies in a millennium of sand.
Windswept dunes preserve the fantail, the wings.
The shaman's plane is lost, Arafat assumed dead.
The women have lived with the wind for centuries.
They are accustomed to the blood-rain, remnants.
In the dried interior lives burn quietly to breathless ends.
Tomorrow, in thirty years, the wreckage will be found.
Sandals will be polished by years of wear.
Goatskin cases of notes are worthless as Dead Sea Scrolls.
The image is perfectly preserved at a starboard window.
Here are the presumptions and blessings of Chubab.
But the wind circles the camp like an unkind consort.
Birth is not easy here, nor death.
Years of fire and sand will not assuage the Simoom.
Where Arafat should be, a burnouse, upright, unmoved.
Thirty years of fire have not assuaged the Simoom.

Hesitations

The women's hands are dusted with flour.
They understand the reflections in the oasis spring.
Birth is not easy here, nor the terror of red dust on the wind.
Their camp fires burn down, the wind quiets.
In sleep they embrace a millennium of dunes.
No beast with lion's head stirs beneath the sand.
The wings, the fuselage, the fantail, are preserved.
No beast will rise to slouch toward Bethlehem.
By midnight the sky is clear.
The women lift their faces to the stars.
Tomorrow is thirty or a thousand years.
History, seeking respite, uncovers the wreckage.
The Simoom has written a history of loss.
At a starboard window, they find a burnouse, upright.
Sandals have been polished by years of wear.
Goatskin cases of notes remain unopened.
The women wrap their Abayas to their thighs.
They turn away from fires to a distant lament.
The oppressive prophecy of the Simoom.
If Arafat is never found, he will be with them, tomorrow.
At al-sooq they hold their skirts tightly to their thighs.
A distant droning of a plane carries far in the night.
If Arafat is never found, he waits for them at al Sahar.

Scribes & Scriptures

On hearing that the penalty for killing
a scribe in eighth century Ireland was
the same as for killing a bishop

before you loose a murderous rage
to send scribes scrambling
with their scribblings or deny
bishops the breath to haul
beginning claims pulpit-ward
or find salvation in death
beware the word you would intend
what word cut short beware what
word is left to law transcribed
in myth for all of what is written
and said is not the same and within
what they embrace cultures can go bad
   in either case the dead do not sing
   and killing is a despicable thing

A Priest Dies an Unnatural Death

First reports place him in the wrong
part of town, an unfortunate turn,
the middle of night, a one-way street

crossing the tracks to the wrong side,
the unacceptable of decayed tenements,
teenage prostitutes, dealers, the bare

earthly siblings of desire and need –
innocent as a child in its mother's arms
is innocent - and all of it a mistake.

Though who's to say in ecumenical rites
how a man of cloth could be thus mistaken?
Should he not have had a universal passport,

territorial immunity, safe passage to instinct,
even in darkness a rightful place in whatever
place he chose? Of course, theories abound.

Dismas in the catacombs, mistaken identity.
Then in a day more sordid insinuations,
accusations, information gleaned in a glance,

the cold and staring eyes of a police blotter,
the coroner's evidence: sex. Sex, he had
vowed to forsake, forever, as if ever there

was such a time or man to do such a thing.
That night an unrepentant Magdalene,
(the story is loaded with Biblical implications),

her cloak spread on the backseat, dollars
exchanged, her shadowed pimp waiting,
maybe Barabbas, obvious corollaries.

It's easy to imagine Christ poorly dressed
among the lepers or lacking a special gown
for raising Lazarus. And then the mysteries

of an unnatural demise at the hands of inhumanity,
his and theirs, of being neither here
nor there, fish nor fowl, in an unfortunate

night or disparate town – his Roman collar
missing, promises unlikely to be kept,
vows broken, respectability tainted, a special

retribution for his part in the failing scheme
of things – and three deadly nails, three bullets
hammered in like nails into a priestly head.

Letters from Bucharest

You write from Bucharest each spring,
and maybe three or four times in between,
Par Avon. Shadowing the personal,
the optimistic lines shield an inner-voice

speaking a nation of woe. The days lift
and fall like gentle breezes, somehow
out of focus, beyond reach, to comfort,
refresh, edify or mark the steady going

on of a way of life. Each fall I fashion
answers, an observation or two about
society and sex, replies, and in due time
send them to you – the russet, yellow

notebook leaves. But that's the way of
our connections. Lands traveled by
months of waiting. The postman walks
a tree-lined street with a Roman tongue.

Who will open your mail?

Breaking & Entering

Tonight the burglar will be a woman
who comes by way of a bedroom
window, not so much in evening
as the darkest dead of night.

Within the Common Law that's how
it has to be: to *break* and *enter*
the *dwelling* of *another* at *night*
intending to *committee a felony.*

Breaking in may be the hardest part,
to slip past Cerberus, three heads,
six eyes to watch the glowing night.
And then the distance of the sill

from ground up, to enter over
pointed shrubs and mirrored
storm windows reluctant to give up
protecting against the rain and wind.

One hand up, two over the sill,
to ease open the sash, then a foot,
patient human-spider crawling
into the dim night-light of the room,

a dwelling of accessories collected,
she imagines, for someone just like her,
a clock-face glowing with luminescent
hands and fragrances of emollients and

colognes, the soft pad of absorbent
carpet stealing the sound of everything
but the sleeping deep breathing lifting
from the bed, there for the taking.

Primavera

she appears at first to be alone
a moss-green uniform
hip-length top and scrub-pants
auburn hair to the middle of her back
well situated beyond the signs
disclaiming alcohol and litter
harassing park participants
in a grove of budding saplings

you wonder what she is up to
on a spring day
hovered over a winter-weathered table

until the details
the twitch of shoulders
her hands out of sight
betray the partner she fondles
as a nurse might
with great care

she straightens slowly
stares into open spaces
beyond the trees
the tennis court and soccer fields
as if surveying her domain
to the waterfall-pool
lovers fill each spring with detergent
to flood the banks with billowing white foam
to a distant periphery of jogging track
where runners circle like satellites

and satisfied that all is well
she slips her scrubs to the knees
exposing massive buttocks
bare Botticelli white-flesh legs
moist stumps recently peeled of bark
her enormous pale stomach
framed in a deep patch of greenery

she leans toward the table
hesitates for adjustments
to assure the efficiency of the enterprise
ready as if she could then

embrace the entirety of the blue-planet
the reasons for pain and illness
and food and love with seas and fishes
wild and mad animals in tides and storms
to take it all in her fleshy arms
squeeze it into her corpulent body

oblivious of man's hectoring prohibitions
with a personal passion for nurturing
she lifts herself rising on tip-toe
bounces slightly to shake the table
the earth beneath it a bit
and after a short while she makes an end
at least for the time

with a nonchalance regarding the confines
her miniature garden this paradise
she rearranges her hauteur
repositions her clothing

Hesitations

and with something of aplomb
exits the grove
hand in hand with a man
hardly half her size

Wayne Lanter

Chicken Soup

There's a thing women have
about chicken soup
when they are feeling subservient
as all hell and don't want to mess
with the peculiarities of sex.
It has to do with food
serving a primary appetite.
Sex is something you do to kill time,
and the ingredients on the can
are labeled "this is what he likes,"
without thinking it through

though what he really likes is not soup at all
but having some under-thing at his command,
a prostitute or politician
cooking or bowing down or jumping
through burning hoops
to get to the stove.

But when the soup is gone, the pot cooled,
and they try to write a poem,
it comes out brittle and sharp,
all quills, claw-feet, beaks and backbone,
and they wonder for weeks after
why they feel disgusted at the sight
of a chicken, naked or alive.

Room 3124 - Bed #1

Old Adam Lampman calls out in the night.
He calls to nurses who have gone off shift,
the nameless clerks he bullied in his store
for years, and for his wife gone decades, now.
During the day he dozes in a room
of white, a yarmulke fit to his head
like a beret, connecting times and places
past where all must come to grief or rest.
For eighty years he's clung to his beliefs,
observing the Sabbath, the festivals,
the fasts, though now it seems unlikely
that in the end they will provide for him.
 He calls into a night with no one there,
 reducing sight and insight to a stare.

Eve

At seventy she's shriveled down to nothing
but six kids two husbands in the dust of failing crops
and worries if there'll be enough to eat.
All she recalls of childhood is rabbit stew and
cornbread three times a day amid a land of plenty
where farms stretched from the edge of town
out to infinity. They had four rooms a small yard
for nine of them to learn to give in and though
the pacific appear weak and sad mocking the illusion
of servitude she knows that to serve servants
must be fed. At night she listens to the news
crime reports and weather but refuses to drive in rain.
  She hands a tray of fruit across the table now
  certain that even here plenty will fail somehow.

Seeing Wordsworth in London

And all around a whirl of debris
from Russell Square to the Thames.
A theme of spirits roams the street
where lamp-posts seared by flames
provide a second-sight, give up
their thick black paint in small degrees.
The close and deadly air shrouds
those who would, if only they could,
escape to the hills.
Yet nothing much has changed this day,
of how we think or what we feel.
And William mingles with the crowd,
meeting face to face his Mass of human-kind.
A bundle of *The Philanthropist*
beneath his arm, he looks and ceases not
to look for mysteries one might discover
in the light of stolen fire. Discerning
phantasms of heart from unmoved man,
he seems not to understand
the artless hands that sculpt these forms.
He dreams a city to life, a soul devoid of habit.
We are beggars-all at heart,
slouched against the wall, with blinded stories
to tell, the spirit of riot and public hangings,
of desire twisted without redemption.
The written papers round our necks
are scrawled with the platitudes of shades
and shifters – all we know of ourselves

or of the universe – like seeing him,
in these advanced decades,
among the heat and blowing debris,
consumed with a desire for release,
devoid still of ennobling harmony.

Hesitations

After the Game

He's lifted in the seventh
two hits, a stolen base,
already dressed when the team
comes in. The elder statesman,
kidding the rookies.
After twenty years of seasons
he lives a moment of triumph.
Today is today, and tomorrow?
There will be time to . . . .
He has seen the footman
holding the coat to his career,
of a man years ago
on a journey begun on a day
nearly now lost to memory.
He will walk the last few miles,
base to base to the dugout.
When day is done,
the clubhouse is empty.
Tomorrow he will begin again,
then on another day . . . .

Wayne Lanter

Bad Choices

It took fourteen years
to get him back,
what was left
after the capture, torture, the killing.
Fourteen years for a box of bones,
medallions, an insignia – maybe
a belt buckle and dog tags.

His son was three at the time –
seventeen when they returned the remains,
though not at all what a three-year-old
would have had in mind –

always waiting for the phone to ring,
the doorbell,
at the bus stop
waiting
to see if, just possibly,
there might be one more person off.

You wonder what he hoped to leave.
A stack of ribbons, medals,
commendations,
an inflated biography?
We are all better the day after.
A hundred years from now,
tomorrow,
nobody cares.

Hesitations

But what about today?
Maybe we should treat them better,
leave more to remember,
make better choices for our sons.

Boise City

founded on fraud going west
the roads leading to the City
are traumatized by broken homes
and pivot-spiders sucking life
from playas and aquifers
feeding an eternity of crop-cycles
that feed no one

solitary ring-necked pheasants
run for their lives like road-runners
hoping to make it to the other side

and signs in the Best Western
presage a hefty fine
for cleaning a bird in your room

to protect the innocent
pending notification
the prairie chicken
duck
woodcock
at issue is not named
though that's to be expected

once upon a time
rain did not drop from the sky
and dust farmers threw into the sky
rolled over the land
like a man-made tsunami
further complicated the scam

Hesitations

one night in '43
a star-crossed B-17 crew
on a practice bombing run
confused the village square for a target

it didn't harm anything
except the town
the second time in a decade

the story goes
in the Best Western
that the bird (the prairie chicken duck
woodcock at issue) came to life
somewhere in the second quarter
between Seattle and Atlanta
or maybe Baltimore and Arizona
somewhere near the middle
of a second six-pack
and all-too-frequent back-slaps

in the middle of the game
the reclassified assumed-dead bird
(still anonymous)
took to broken flight
veering from ceiling
to window and wall
pushing the brown paper wrapper
painting blood-stars
on the early evening
of the white Western wall skyline

there were feather-smeared nebulae
above the flat-screen
a dozen or so Red Dwarfs
and a couple crimson-clawed Quasars
in a deep space to the right of the door

of course the resuscitation
prompted warnings
though in a Best Western fabrication
covering the splatters and smears
the stacks of sucked-up
and bombed-out rubble

decades later neither the pilots
nor the hunters would comment
and no one knows the condition
of the bird
or if it made it to the other side

Hesitations

Looking into the Millennium

There was a dozen of them or so
depending on who you want to believe
though their number had diminished
of late lazing about killing time
in a dim barred room not entirely fearful
with plenty of wine and a feast on the table
that no one had bothered with

three were in one corner shooting craps
one dozed in an erotic fantasy
of Mary's pulchritude in her bath
another picked the pale peeling skin
from his withered hand
another crouched in the passage
leading to the chained door
mumbling to himself about his ill-fate

four or five others washed in the gray light
of the cruciform balistrariae
of their self-imposed sarcophagus
sat on the dirt floor staring at the stone walls
wondering what to do next
wondering what would become of them

if in their thoughts they were confounded
by what they had just seen and heard
as if from nowhere or at least out of
the grey mist they gathered around them
not one at a time though possibly
one or two stirred before the others

as one they rose and stood squinting
into the haze at the aspect
appearing in the musk out
of a farther wall of human misery
and wailing that roiling throng of flesh
making its way into the desert
and each stretched out an arm a hand
not necessarily to touch
but possibly to regain his balance
to correct his vision
to understand having seen so much
of something he could not touch

A Found Poem

She writes to tell me
She has found a poem
Tucked in the pocket of an old coat
As threadbare as iambic lines
And wonders if it is mine
Did I leave it? Did I write it?

I write to tell her otherwise
It would not have been there
I abandoned it with the insinuations
One might hope for or imagine
Though there will never be enough
In what blind fingers find
In the dark I had hoped
To caress the frayed threads
The pocket in the poem
The deeper creases
We too often leave undone
To turn the better parts
Of fortune our way

Wayne Lanter

You Had to Suspect

it is good the world series is over
for a time it seemed no one would win

the stars did not shine brightly
the worried fanatics turned in their seats
to search the horizon for a new day

in three billion years the sun collapsed
and no one in the stadium had found
an answer the final score the final out

might give and so the pitcher took
the mound and the hitter showed up
with his bat – a different hitter

each millennium or so – at many points
they ran out of umpires and strikes
were no longer called as balls floated

away in the ether until it all came
together again and somehow at the crack
of the bat somebody connected on a long one

and somebody didn't catch the thing and
the scoreboard lit up like a constellation
and the stars expanded into stellar space

it is good the world series is over
for a time it seemed no one would win

Disappearing

I've practiced disappearing
a little at a time hearing sight

the fallible taste and touch
they say your sense of smell
is last to go
Snodgrass' dandruff on the tabletop
Eliot's infamous month breeding Lilacs

a senior moment (a cliché)
turns into an hour glass on its side
the sand divided
time still ticking in the grain

I'll drive north
to the small towns
of Cognito and Visible
I have friends there
who do not mind my disappearance
a few in Cognito a few in Visible –
they will take me in

English Class

we meet like this every other day
and will for sixteen weeks missing only
an occasional session before the room
and the cluster we constitute disappears

a hundred years from now no one will know
or care about what we did or whether
we were at the window regarding
spring trees budding or near the door

prepared to retreat the words we utter
in exasperation or love are not recorded
by any means to be preserved or remembered
and referred to by future generations

hoping to find wisdom or consolation
in the sounds our ideas make in meeting
like this every other day persistently

Sobriety Check Points

Maybe a favorite child suffering a harmless
seizure pulls you off the street, pushes you
into a parking lot in the middle of the night,
with others, the chosen few, selected at random.

Amid a host of flashing lights, maybe the voice
of a lover, dead for twenty years, wakes you,
the whine caged like canines shepherded
by uniformed skinheads carrying paraphernalia

designed to test your faculties and estimate
the merit of the choices you have made. Whatever
the task, you are never prepared to walk straight
lines on command or stand on one leg and count

from a hundred to seventy-five or to jump into
the alphabet as if it was a marked course and recite
the monotonous sing-song to the end. Everything's
arranged for failure: the time (just to this or that

side of midnight) the slope of asphalt (laid out
for proper drainage) chosen by people who feed
on the mistakes of others. You suspect you have
not been sober enough, too often entertaining

the intoxications of fictions, how things appear,
that you have been naive about the nature of nature,
have forgotten that once you believe in something
that is not there, it is only a short step to not believe

in what is. When all is done and you slip free
you do not even bother to ask why the dogs
are kept in cages or why the exhaust and red lights
are so dead-determined to assail the unwary.

Walking Home

Abandoned to life and night consumed
in raptures of what cannot be undone like Sartre's
authentic man you accept the hazards of darkness
commanding the right lane on the Martin Luther King
bridge walking with your back to traffic a Bible
cradled like a child in your arms crossing a proverbial
River Jordan not walking on water but over it
with Kierkegaard's infamous leap from anguish
to another the only passage available tail-lights
snaking by dividing destiny and fate as the Red Sea
was divided if for a time the Word appears to rise
and float in the spots of light the casinos cast on water
    when they find your body those miles down stream
    the Logos in flesh is still an unreadable broken dream

Walking on Lake Erie
for Robert Stephens (1941-2009)

My first reaction would have been
    to say "Don't do it," but
I wasn't there that winter night

of wind, ice, the lake frozen
    a mile or so beyond the shore.
"It took six weeks to freeze.

It always does," you said,
    "and one night in the moonlight
we walked out onto the ice sheet."

The ice was a foot thick, a new
    crust, with little chance
of breaking through to the singularity

of deep-black water from which
    nothing can return. "Yet, some things
do return," you said. "Why just

the other day a woman, missing
    all summer, washed ashore among
the driftwood and smooth stones."

The water had removed her clothing
    and bathed the body. Still, I wonder
why you want to walk where the footing

Hesitations

is treacherous or faulty, at best. I would
   tell you to avoid that blanched and
tortured landscape of powdered snow

dusting the ice, the evening bright,
   enough to see all the way home,
the soft light of windows on the shore

carrying sound for miles. Standing
   in silence, smoking a cigarette,
its fires aglow, at fifteen below,

surveying this newest territory
   you said you knew the lake was
in a nasty mood. You could hear it

grumbling of the trespass. It had
   talked to you before. Then the ice
began to crack, far out, at first, fissures

popping like rifle shots, racing toward
   you, passing at light-speed,
a near miss in the pale, dim night.

We need to read the ice. Nothing
   came apart that night. At least for a time,
things remained in place, a giant puzzle

in a giant frame. But as usual, there is
   always more. We do not see how
we hold together, why and how our feet

grip where we stand, what brings light
    to our eyes when we lose sight,
what binds and keeps the stars from flying

apart or from coagulating to a black mass
    heavier than god. Winter nights
the lake's gigantic fluid-eye watches and

waits beneath a frozen lens, a companion
    universe reflecting just enough
intelligence to remind us it is there. And so

I would tell you to avoid that sacred
    water, roiling on itself, waiting
for the equinox to shake its joints loose,

jealous of arrangements with the flow
    of things, casting lots for our
tattered garments, intending to restate

the uncompromising rules of nature
    and/or mind in a quantum leap
we partially intuit but never understand.

Love's Forgiveness

My love you say "After all,"
and I interrupt
as I always do,
knowing well this may displease you,
yet hoping not to hear
what I have feared, and so
must risk again to quiet
the lips I love, the lips I have kissed
that have kissed me,
and so must chance again

to find distress that tells me
the soul I long to touch has turned away,
clouded and closed.

So after all is said and done, after all
this time, I wait for you to tell me
"After all, this is the end, I am through."

And then, following a terrible pause you say,
"Yes, after all I have done to you,
forgive me." Yes, after all.

Samhain Eve, Nearing Midnight

and I wonder what ghosts are loose
that might have frequented me
and my privy domain
god forgive them
those I have loved and wronged
who have wronged and loved me

you see the cemetery
is a block away
and I was married once
on All Saints' Day
divorced on the day of all souls
when the tormented are ushered into heaven
or so the story goes

the anniversary
that beginning of winter and chaos
of entering
with purgatory's yellow lanterns
glowing like pumpkin eyes
of the unrepentant
hovering silent as bats on wing
ominous as owls
in branches of stripped trees
or on blank stones
waiting for names and dates
a grinning jack-o'-lantern mask

the time of desire and fear
crawls from the body's crypt

Hesitations

to wander restlessly
beneath the moon
its candle nearly out
but still flickering

Marriage

These were people who would not
agree on anything, even after

thirty-three years, not on why
they married or whether they

should have. He claimed he nixed
the idea without saying why

he changed his mind or how
in objecting he said "I do,"

although he did. She disagreed.
One thing she knew, she said,

after all the years, was that he
was wrong. And then the small things.

He drank too much, smelled up
the house with bad cheese and

herring (as opposed to cigars and socks)
and was nowhere nearly as kind

as her father. To his view she never
did cook as well as his mother.

When she balanced the checkbook
it never came out right. And don't

bother talking numbers, adding
and multiplication, that had nothing

Hesitations

to do with it. And so on into another
angry silence, drawn out, prolonged

for maximum effect, until the day
he required heart surgery when

nothing was certain save the chance
of failure itself. A grown daughter,

suggested she (Mom) avoid the hospital,
not complicate his convalescence

with bickering. The bitter words
chilled the air. At the mere suggestion

questioning her sense of duty,
she froze into an armored stance,

her anger so thorough, so perfect
and absolute that all the years

of discord, spiked with rancor
as they were, paled to the merest

ghost of a sun, which everyone
appreciated for having been there.

American Night

> at each streetlight
> i am tempted
> to kneel and pray
>
> down the darkened lonely street
> one by one
> like stations of the cross
>   American Night – Chuck Miller

I know exactly what you mean.
Maybe Durante closing out the show.
It's the quintessential American scene.

In the first spot of light it would seem
he's at the end, with no place to go.
I know exactly what you mean.

He tips his hat to his good luck, the dream
of millions watching him. We know,
it's the quintessential American scene.

A moment later he vanishes between
the spots, then reappears, still, not wanting to go.
We know exactly what you mean.

So from spot to spot he crosses the screen,
from spot to spot into the darkness beyond the show.
It is the quintessential American scene.

Then the "Goodnight Mrs. Calabash," unseen,
as the final "wherever you are." Both apropos.
Yes, I know exactly. What you mean,
it is the quintessential American scene.

Hesitations

The Stone in the Road

The story goes that three weeks
    following the twister that rolled
it down the hill, the rock, boulder,

stone, whatever you want to call it,
    stayed in the middle of Douglas
Road, its presence stimulating if not

demanding speculation and debate.
    Some said the hand of God had
put it there, which at its root and for

a time seemed reasonable. At twenty
    hands, it stood a foot taller than
the tallest man. It's weight and density

could hardly be imagined. So dwarfed
    were ideas by the size, the practicalities
of moving it, there could be only vague

circumspection, little invention, and
    all of it without a wit of spiritual
enterprise. Of course, as always

believers did not want to tamper
    with what they deemed God had
done. Others, infected with Blaise's

wager, did not wish to risk the chance.
    But those possessed of a more
earthly bent, intending to reclaim

the road, contrived how it might be
    lifted and transported. Still, it stayed
hard in the roadway and in a matter

of days a bow of tracks circled it
    to either side. Then one morning
a month or so later a band of miners

from the Eden mine patch gathered
    with hammers and star bits. Working
in shifts, that day, and another, to pack

the holes with dynamite, as they say,
    borrowed, from the Red Ray mine,
the third day they stretched a detonating

cord beyond the hill and with everyone
    warned, fired the charge sending
a flare of fire and pebble shards

a thousand feet into the air, causing
    a minor meteor shower. The rumble
rolled out across the countryside. Three

miles away windows rattled and china
    fell from shelves. For half an hour
it snowed dust. But looking over the hill,

to see what they had done, prepared
    for the cleanup, their expectation quieted
and stilled. For at the core of what had

Hesitations

blocked the road, its outer layers split
    away and crumbled, standing upright
and haughty against the odds, they found

the solitary figure of a man of stone.
    Sculpted to a single image by the blast,
as if he had been there, always, waiting

and certain he would be freed, he endured
    the fire, the explosion, the sole survivor
of a universe of possibilities, the debris

and dust of whatever else there could
    have been now at his feet, remarkable
and accidental as anything in Genesis.

What the Dead Say

This is not Lady Lazarus
come back to say "and I shall tell you"
but the dead seeing the wind
with one wide blue eye
speaking softly in their silence
about their failed misgivings.

This is Houdini squirming
in his twisted cage of softened steel
shrouded by the falling dust of trust
and disbelief.

This is the entire Lazarus family
trying to right itself
again and again
a vaudeville troupe
a legion of jugglers
and quick-change escape artists
caught without clothes on the street
unzipping their skins and stepping out
its theater a pile of rubble
ascribing to the good luck of miracles
attempting to avoid the inevitable.

These are stone masons
lifting the vaulting at Beauvais
in the difficulty of telling
what will stand or fall
a small step from believing in what is
to seeing what is not.

Hesitations

This is what the dead see.

The body count will continue.
The Lazarus family works the balance beam
without their skins
hoping no one will notice.
There is no clear reason why they do this.
But this is what the dead say
when they have anything at all to say.

Wayne Lanter

The Poet Alone in the End
For Valeda Evans (1905-2000)

She came to this at the end,
in the sun near an open window,

unable to hear the children
playing in the street or see

a tasteless world, the deep green
park devoid of touch, well

beyond a second childhood.
Innocent still, she complained.

Bifocals and hearing aids
failed to alter her perceptions.

It was not so much reversal
as discovery. Each day she

turned a little, as a space-craft
losing contact, profoundly

alone in space, might make
an enormous soft arc towards

a gravitational field
it had abandoned. Slowly,

her hands, grown small by then,
and memories, the details she

47

Hesitations

rehearsed for a century, were
no longer what she recalled.

She did not grieve a lost husband.
Twenty-odd years soothed by

the balm of bereavement
left her more than sympathetic.

To apprehend his impending
presence she fashioned a sharp

self-indulgence. Childbirth,
for example, unlike what

she recalled, was in dwindling
pain fraught with pleasure,

and sons she imagined into life,
passed, themselves, into anticipation.

Little by little her lines unraveled
from pages that hardened into wood.

Even the sun receded until she
could no longer see or hear the children

or touch the tasteless world,
where insight slips to senselessness.

So once again she was, as she
had been before, without hands

to hold the celebrations
of a world unwinding into

a single cell, turning slowly,
coming to this, in the end.

Migration

They never thought it through or wrote it down.
They had no blueprint for excess or fear.
Yet they flew nearly perfect patterns
stacked against the sky
row on row headed for paradise
in early fall a land of palms
dreaming in the sun *where money*
out-weighs the next best thing.

To them it was no more Eden
than any other place.
Of course they did not know this
drifting slightly to the right responding
only to a biology that lifted them
into the wind *drifting* south *today*
or *tomorrow* north.

You see it was not misguided passion.
They lived with the pepper-shot
of misfortune mistaking a reflection
in the lake for the sky in their eyes.

And when they died, they died wide-eyed
with surprise and fell straight down
as if the sky-scrapper currents
of the lives they rode and all the energy
collected into matter had warped space
leaving nothing to hold on to
dropping down, dropping down.

The Poetry Reading
for John K & Jim S

at end of the long corridor
    where man waits in a nearly empty theatre
    words filling the hollow spaces
    with echoes more pronounced than gifts
when the lights come on
    waiting for the guests to arrive
    with slow words I introduce the poet
    who steps forward
    and says of me "that old white-haired man
    was a student of mine"
    we met at 7:30 in the morning
    a great class but that was long ago
I remember
    a new child then
    that barely made it in
    a doubtful child
    grown now with blue eyes
    to see clearly words
    articulated in careful syllables
    but that too was long ago
the video
    is a documentary
    not about a poet's life but poetry
    criers sent out to invite guests to hear Sophocles
    and see the river-shots
    of rituals from the banks
    blessing the blessed life-giving waters
    a boat pushing great weights
    against the current

Hesitations

    the poet's voice over it all
    the constant waters lapping the shore
at the reading
    the poet steps off screen
    to greet would-be-guests
    who ignore the invitation
    not knowing the poetry in vows
    the power of sacraments
    when poets read
in conclusion
    there is a great danger here
    as Merwin says despite magic
all of us may be lost
    ferried over another river
    to a darkened ancient world
    of echoes and silences
    forgetting to see and feel
    the next generation

The Poetry Bowling Contest

Thirty of them show up, give or take a few,
depending on the day, day-dreaming,
drugs, excitement, on who comes
through the spinning glass doors, etc.

And for the most they stand around
waiting for the lights to brighten,
the Brunswick automatics to lift,
the reactive balls to clack in bent racks.

Some have nimble fingers, nails chewed
down to the quick. Some glare in the dim light.
Others' hands are knotted in gripping gloves.
Others squint to see to the far end of the alley.

In an uncoordinated parade of human frailty
those with braced-legs lurch toward the words,
those with weak hands fumble the words,
stiff fingers embrace the round black words.

Some have no sense of direction.
Others seem not to know how they got here.
Some cradle the ball in their happenstance.
Others use unorthodox approaches,

sometimes holding the word with both hands,
other times rolling it softly in a mind-set,
somehow, that will not insure success.
Others, are wheeled up in large chairs,

Hesitations

Words are committed to halting steps,
lines of zigzagging balls clattering on wood,
stanzas that do not add up to much of anything –
cantos beautifully but poorly written.

Others utilize a device aimed somewhat
at centering the words on the lane.
Others do not bowl at all but watch.
Some imagine. But that, too, is a contest.

Keeping it all out of the gutter is not
possible. In the fifth frame a rumor
circulates. Ten lanes up the line someone
got a strike. No one has picked a spare.

By now the score keeper has given up.
It's too much trouble when everyone
is winning, when everyone is satisfied
and certain that they, too, will make a strike.

An hour later it all looks perfectly normal.
Still, fifty feet or so away in the balance
at the edge of the pit the mystery remains
of why some things fall and others stand.

Wayne Lanter

Getting to the Dance

She's twelve, one year
for each member of the jury,
the months, the apostles.

Six months ago she had a period,
a trial run, a female exercise
to check-out things, just in case.

Nothing since. And sometimes
it's all gloom, a temperament
she wears like a new pair of shoes.

Otherwise, she's in her room
bunched-up on her bed
buried in a pile of homework,

wrestling fractions of a world
to come, graphs for the height
and density of stars or reading

The Cask of Amontillado,
her eyes wide. "I called aloud, Fortunato –"
tracking clues from Forensic Files.

The prickled spines of pop-songs,
pin-clipped glossies of anorexic
females, muscular, fuzzy males

Hesitations

hang on the bedroom walls.
Mid-afternoon she gets
into a one-on-one basketball

scrap at the Y, a kid her age
named Jamal. He's quicker, stronger,
something she hasn't experienced,

a time to make adjustments.
She leans on him, pushes him out
to mid-court. No man's land.

Hits a couple hard shots,
near the end, comes out of it
puffing, red-faced two points

down. He loops his arm
around her shoulder, leans on her,
both of them tired. She grins and

says. "How'd I do?" and on the way home
talks about the school dance
that night, about her overweight

friend, Ben, his enmity
for a step-mom with big tits,
holds out her tee-shirt

with her fingers, "Out to here,"
she looks down, says, "Wow,"
talks about Ben's joke of lacing

stepmother's Chanel with vinegar.
Ben doesn't like music, thinks
sports are silly – Ben who . . . well,

it's difficult to predict. Later
they bicycle into a foreign
neighborhood and Ben disappears,

abandons her. Not yet a true-believer
she finds her way back seriously pissed.
"Asshole," she says, "just

left me there, without a map."
Before the dance, in a new
knee-length dress, on her bed,

legs up she trims her toenails,
her white panties shining
in the dark room. That night

she dances all the dances
with Ben who'd like to dance
with another girl, but won't ask.

"Other boys are out to see how
many girls they can get," she says.
"But not Ben. He isn't like that."

Chicago Nocturne – 1964

I
As a rule, people like to travel to the top
of things, the Statue of Liberty,
the Washington Monument, the Sear's Tower.
When we were young with money enough
we'd take the elevator up countless floors
to the Sea Gull restaurant on Lake Shore Drive.
For an extra five you could get a table
facing the river, the lake, tankers at anchorage,
the mist of Gary's shore beyond,
headlights moving silently
between parallel pearl strings of street lamps
along the Drive. The soft candle flame
in glass, deep in the city would hold
the darkest nights at bay.
We knew the dangers of the insolence,
even then, intersecting migration patterns,
how life is undermined,
a temporary thrill of borrowed time,
and each of us a limited edition, a fad.

II
We cherished the sensation of being greater
than we were, above it all, easy to imagine
what royalty must feel, removed from earth
and people, apart from the needs of the unborn
or the newly dead, avoiding what we are
and cannot help but be. We needed to pretend,
even if for a moment, our pretense
encased in glass like an ancient artifact,
overlooking a well-lighted night.

III
When it rains the streets glisten.
Someone some place must know
how the city runs – those who stay up
to keep the lights burning.
The Irish politicians on South Lowe
remember horse drawn days and what remains
from a time when coal was delivered
by mule cart and shovel – when their fathers
drove steel casings into bedrock.
Black women move through the dark rain
to police stations to ransom their men.
An ounce of crack will not replace painful
memories or seal the roach holes in the walls.
Small children disappear into the cracks
and sink into the quicksand at Oak Street beach.
Gangs roam the perimeters of night,
waiting for a chance meeting.
New technologies forget old ways.
Whole cities disappear. And people.
Greek restaurants feature sushi and kishke.

IV
The city rumbles underground.
Who would have thought of voyages
deeper than the River Styx? Does a labyrinth
of passages lie beneath river
for reluctant souls to drop out of the oarsman's boat?
We will need maps to show the manholes,
set like mines in the streets,
that drop into the subterranean chambers
beneath Drexel and Buckingham fountains.

Hesitations

V
We take the elevator to the top for a better view.
The rain on the window frames the candle flame.
A waiter carries a white serviette on his arm.
We will wait for the river, the city, to vanish.

Motherhood

She buried seven of them,
secretly as deadly sins or sorrows,
one a seventh son of a seventh son,
a seer without fore- or hindsight,
muscling myth against myth
into a backyard of strange sheds
set on concrete slabs.

One sheltered shovels and rakes,
two held shadows, a small one,
in the far corner, always locked,
harbored the panic of nocturnal planting,
its interior arranged with antiquated lamps,
though none to illuminate her reasons.

Aware that nurturing is a spectator sport
negotiated for money, fame, love,
or maybe righteous indignation,
played underground rules
for a practice none dare criticize,
she administered to the elderly, the lame,
and disenfranchised, she had taken
under wing, honoring the maternal twist
on which she fed –
so long as their benefits arrived on time.

And when they did not,
she dispatched them,
the errant ones, swaddled and stitched
cocoon-like, in canvas and blankets
and disdain, with something of aplomb.

Hesitations

When asked, she led the police
to her garden nursery of monuments
granting them concession to excavate.
While they dug, to avoid the acclaim
her maternal nurturing might gather,
she ventured off to a coffee shop –
and disappeared, prepared
to advance her lethal fostering
at another venue, then another.

A Small Response

She writes from across town
　　to say she's doing well

at ninety-one chides me about
　　the way I dress

says I look better without
　　a beard and adds she's still

writing poetry finding a place
　　to put an unaccented

foot in front of another though
　　I hear otherwise

from relatives hers not mine
　　who say she's clearing

out the house giving away things
　　she took years to find

a use for closing the circle
　　as her senses falter

her hearing fades, her sight and
　　hindsight failing

with intimations of what is
　　to come in silence

the motionless dust extended
　　into the giant web

Hesitations

on the farther wall she will pass
    and I wonder

how I might reply with words
    in a hand drawn

script reaching across the span
    of our ages bearing

condolences the small response
    to a condition

not to be assuaged with adages
    homilies clichés or poetry

A Crossroad in Samaria

I found a woman in the sand.
People were everywhere,
but no one offered or extended a hand.
And to tell the truth, neither did I.
I had seen this kind of thing before —
her sandals worn in peculiar ways
from walking among the ruins.
The dress that should have covered her
was soiled and torn.
She had sand in her hair,
more than likely from the fall
from the rocks stacked beside the road
where she tried to hide her despair.

What is the balance we seek?
Learning to fall may be the best we can do.

Yet, she seemed not to have begun life,
but by most appearances appeared
middle-aged. Someone said
she failed at everything she tried.
What else might be of note only time will tell.

So I turned away, as did others,
though they were more vehement than I.
Some shook their heads and motioned
with their hands that it would be
ill-advised to offer her comfort or aid.
And for a moment I agreed.
Though even with my reasons
it all seemed strange.

Poverty

I

Today I saw a woman searching for a man.
Though, easily it could have been
the other way. She looked in all the places

people are wont to look. I tell you this
because there are so many and it is so
difficult to know where to begin, or how

to end. She thought perhaps an open field,
below the tree line, where nothing grows
but dandelions and blankets of winter snow

among the hope that openness gives. But
the path leading in led out into a cemetery
of tilted stones. She tried a supermarket

where things mephitic and sweet
are packaged to perfection. One day she
ended in a church, between the altar and

the choir. Once, I heard a friend tell of
a Sunday morning sun angled in stained
glass. Candles and incense burning,

an organ with voices in a Mozart
requiem, small bells, and large,
ringing. An imitation pieta at the door

welcomed her. She even thought to search
the sacristy, where people sometimes
take sanctuary. Another morning she

gazed into the bathroom mirror. After
all, he kept his razor and cologne there.
But the glass was cracked, the light

much too severe with more distortion
than she could manage or believe. I do
not know how long she searched. Or if

anyone offered aid. Eventually she
ended on stage. And although the hours
were long and nights late, she had plenty

of work. Off days she modeled discarded
costumes, reciting worn-out lines as if
they were new. One night she stood in

for Lady Macbeth, another night for Blanche.
Twice, maddened, she tried to sacrifice her
children. Once for money, once for revenge.

II
The farmer down the road understands
the season's rhymes. Says it's in his nature
and the nature of farming. And for all of it

he has a scheme. Years repeat themselves
with regularity, trees grow from trees,
and weeds must be avoided. His overalls

Hesitations

are stitched onto his skin, his neck a red
mutation of the sun and wind. Yes,
he wears a straw hat, and when he speaks

of weather he knows when it will rain,
how to watch for a dog eating grass
or to count the rings around the moon.

To protect yourself from lightning
you will need to capture thunder in a glass,
though thunder sours milk. A train

whistling from the south brings the sound
of rain. Animals running wild in a field
portend a storm. Pigs carrying twigs presage

a cold snap. Remember, he says,
to plant according to the moon, observe
the solstice, and harvest with the sun.

Be mindful of broken mirrors, aware that
standing ladders bespeak misfortune.
You see, there are no schemes for these.

Avert your eyes from a passing train.
Otherwise man needs little. The tree line
marks my property - that's as far as it goes.

He pauses for effect, to clear his mind.
Yes, remember the angel of death
knocks three times and enters once.

III
The south lot stones lean sideways
to the north. Those to the east are cast
another way, their shadowed dates

without regard or quittance for truth.
And though they tell me vandals come here,
I do not think they care about these stones.

Mostly, their hands are small, without
a mind for compilation. Their inclinations
do not lean this way. It is more like trees

edging the sea, unable to move or free
themselves, that must endure eternal
winds and therefore lean together

forever twisted, flat. And though
the stones are set in clay, nothing here
is carved in stone. Care for the graveyard

is paid in perpetuity. On occasion those
who care will come to straighten the stones,
correcting each to an appropriate slant

for the times. One day the graveyard
will be filled with an avalanche of stones.
No one will come with flowers then, or flags.

The vandals are not interested. And finally,
those who care will give in to despair,
their time occupied with games of chance.

Hesitations

This is important to know. Grass grows
thin and very slow, like the hair of the
dead. So upon rising, should there be

a resurrection day, although they will
not recognize the house or road,
the dead will think they are at home.

By then all dates will have weathered
to obscurity, so those arriving in the sun
to trace the angels hovering at the top

will find they have no wings. Stones
stood upright at noon leave no shadow
of what brought them to this place.

Officer Training, 1961

*Even after all the years you still
recall the draft board's finger
on your brow consigning you
to the ranks of Sam's conscripts.*

*Caught in the dilemma of time
and service, to avoid a two-year
incarceration, you capitulate and
sign on with the USMCR, resigned*

*to the anomalies of a ninety-day-wonder.
You find yourself one afternoon
under a sun-drenched blue Virginia sky
in the gravel-lot of grit and grime*

*where buses have dropped you
with other soon-to-be-impressed
civilians – deep within a gray-green
staging ground and Quonset huts.*

*Already training to learn the habit
of getting there on time, you wait
for nine hours, unclaimed – in the land
of good men soaked in humidity.*

*Later, squinting beneath the glare
of floodlights, you wait, thrashed
by New York and Jersey accents
seeking an agreement on the name*

Hesitations

of a ninety-third street deli and
wondering if the bugs (grasshoppers)
in the long grass are flying cockroaches.
You wait until a midnight Sergeant

arrives to welcome you – shit-maggots –
he hopes by the grace of god to turn
into men good enough to face the enemy,
whoever the enemy of the moment might be.

At his command, counting cadence,
he herds you to a warehouse with
cattle stalls from which you emerge
head shaved, strip down, relieved of everything

civil and civilian, to be prodded into the night,
a different self of oversized olives and boots,
a rifle, canteen, haversack, a hundred pounds
of gear to weather whatever atmosphere,

in the requisition of survival that might favor
the luck-of-the-draw – though little sleep.
At dawn you're on the grinder, marching
morning, noon, afternoon, until midnight,

the other half of darkness jumping out,
into and out of your bunk, developing,
as they say, an instinct to obey. You march
without sleep, too exhausted to resist,

until the days are blurred. Then fog-eyed,
one morning in an early mist outside
the mess-hall, waiting, someone
watching the sky mumbles "My God,

Wayne Lanter

look at that!" to the massive water tower
where a platoon of white T-shirts
eighty-feet above the ground,
hangs on the catwalk doing pull-ups.

You can hear their voices on the breeze,
counting, ten, twelve, twenty, thirty.
You wonder how they got there –
how long they can last? When the call

comes you leave them. When you
return, they are gone. Weekend liberty
you drink paper cups of two-percent
at a hut converted to a bar of several

tables, a juke box, cigarette machine
and shuffle board – black and white
photos of Lieutenants, Firsts and Seconds,
on the wall, a prominent pantheon

of those who did not come back.
After taps, a designated Corporal breaks
the silence of the Company street,
an alarm beating a metal garbage can

hung on the head of a hapless recruit
who failed to qualify on the rifle range.
But nothing ever to alter or break the code,
gray as the stones of Wittgenstein's walls.

Quantico

Even after all the years, loathing
seems still too soft a word for what
sticks in your chest when you recall

the draft board's finger on your brow
consigning you to ranks of consecrated
conscripts. An anti-Midas touch, to be

sure, though just as deadly. Twisted
in a nasty dilemma, to avoid a two-year
ordeal of indentured servitude, you

capitulate and sign on with the USMCR,
if not to honor or cherish, at least to obey
for a short time the feral grunts of non-coms

and commissioned cowboys drinking
a manhood withered to the ordination
of death. Out of the blue of a hazy,

sun-drenched Virginia afternoon
you find yourself agape, a gravel-lot
of grit and grime where cattle-carriers

have dropped you. With other
soon-to-be-impressed civilians
deep in the gray-green wilderness

of suicidal orders yet to come,
the staging, assignation ground
and Quonset-hut remains of previous

all too frequent aberrations
you wait – not especially for Godot,
but for someone's inglorious

friend. Already training to get
there on time, at attention, then
parade rest, all but abandoned,

you wait, an alien in the land
of good men – however few – you
wait in the humid night, later

squinting under floodlights that make
the dark darker. You wait, among
the broken chatter of New York,

New Jersey accents arguing
over the name of a ninety-third
street deli, and wondering if

insects diving along the road
are flying cockroaches. You wait
until midnight when a Banty Rooster

sergeant, appears, spic and span
and tucked, well slept, to welcome
you, who he identifies as the slings

and arrows outraged ill-fortune
has cast upon him. *Things,* you are
informed in his short, brutish and nasty

Hesitations

way, that only good luck could turn
into something worthy of defending
his country from a not yet assigned

enemy (a word he uses excessively)
that definition of Hobbesian
first cause intended to excuse

spilling human blood. At his command
you advance into a deeper dimension
of darkness, the sting of his voice

concentrated now on the where
and how of counting cadence
down streets of countless huts,

led to a warehouse resembling
a gas-chamber. Giving up is
followed by giving in, and clipped,

shaved, and stripped down, denuded
of who you might have been,
except for what you are and what

can be taken only by force, you
reappear a divergent-self plucked
from Hume's musings, in oversized

olives and boots, a hundred pounds
or so of gear to weather whatever
atmosphere, where requisition,

living to see another day, favors
nothing if not the luck-of-the-draw.
By dawn you're on the grinder,

marching morning, noon, afternoon,
until midnight, the other half
of darkness spent jumping out and

into and out of your bunk, developing,
as they say, an instinct to obey
any command – the discipline of pain

and discomfort. Twice a week
short-arm-inspections insure
no one has smuggled in contraband

from the contaminated non-military
world. But always marching. Without
sleep, exhausted, unable to resist,

the days blur into a no-beginning,
no-end journey of coming on and
passing off of fields. And frog-eyed,

in an early morning mist of night and
fog outside the mess-hall, rank on rank,
waiting your turn, one, someone or two,

watching the sky, unconvinced as yet
that a new sun might rise, in shallow,
faint disbelief, mumble "My God,

Hesitations

look at that!" You lift your weakened
eyes to the massive water tower
where a squad of white T-shirts flash

eighty-feet above the ground,
hanging on the catwalk, a distant,
string-constellation, doing pull ups.

A moment later their voices ride
in on the breeze, a faint chorus
counting, ten, twelve, twenty, thirty.

You wonder how long they will last
before one falls – when the call comes
you leave them – when you return

they are gone. No one knows to where.
Weekend company liberty at a hut-converted
bar on base you guzzle cups of two-percent,

three tables, a juke box, cigarette machine
and shuffleboard, though less for R & R
than to display the profits of screwing

courage to the insanity of killing and being
killed, surrounded by dozens of black
and white photos of Lieutenants, Firsts

and Seconds who didn't make it. Of course
it all depends on your point-of-view,
which doesn't matter, anyway, since all

are deader than dead as hell, who went
up the hill and came down with nothing
to show but a glossy blank-eyed stare

stuck to an obscure wall, a prominent
pantheon from which none progress
or repair. To give darkness a macabre

twist, after taps the nights are spent
in keeping with the tribal times,
a designated Corporal sullying

the silence of the Company street
with a stick, beating a metal
garbage can hung on the head

of a hapless recruit who failed
to qualify on the rifle range,
yelling to the world of the worn

that "Tonight shit-maggots will pray
for war. Since I ain't had a war
this month. If there ain't war, I'll be

pissed. An' you'd do better to fight
a war than have me pissed." And so
it goes, more of them than of you

by force of law, heredity, the blinding
light of duty wrenched from fantasies
of We. They. Little here of nature

Hesitations

to alter or break the code. Nothing
to question or doubt the darkened logic,
gray as the rot-filled crevices

of Wittgenstein's eternal walls.
The loathing of an invitation
to murder or maim those cast or

claimed as an enemy even when
they have as yet to be chosen
and there is nothing to defend.

Havana, 1958

Even in the early spring Havana was hot.
But the revolution was on so it was dangerous.
Most of the day the ballplayers stayed in their rooms.
They spent only a short time around the pool at the Nacional.
Some of them walked in the well-kept Nacional garden.

The garden was very beautiful and the bay sky-blue.
They leaned over the stone wall and watched the people.
There were six or seven grass huts on bare ground.
Each hut had a dozen or so people but no one said anything.
At four o'clock they rode a bus to Gran Stadium.

The streets were narrow and crowded and old.
Heavy senoras with lace shawls rested on iron balconies.
They waved black handkerchiefs as the players passed.
Two Cubans with a guitar and maracas got on the bus.
They had a deal with the driver and played for the players.

At the stadium they passed the hat.
But some of the players did not give them anything.
The night before they had gone to the Superman Show.
After midnight they found a poker game.
Some of them lost all their money.

Two others fell asleep in a brothel.
The madam called the manager to come and get them.
She was very angry and waved a .45 and shouted.
She was angry and said she could not shoot a sleeping man.
Later the players discovered someone had taken their money.

Hesitations

So some of the players did not have money.
They said the music was no good anyway.
They said the one with the moustache stole from the little
By the fourth the temperature was a hundred and two.
The stands were dark and you could not see the crowd.

They whistled whenever the visiting pitcher took the mo
They had heard rumors about him.
This was before Castro came in from the Sierra Maestra.
Castro wasn't very well known then.
One player said he was a better pitcher than he was a figh

Another said Batista would put down the revolt.
Anyway, Havana was still wide open.
The city was a haven of mafia brothels and casinos.
Businessmen and tourists from Miami frequented the city
During the winter the pitcher had played ball in Havana.

He had gotten a Cuban girl pregnant and it was in the pap
Everyone knew about it and the rumors bothered the Cub
They whistled and cursed the pitcher in Spanish.
Each pitch brought a surge of accusations and insults.
If the pitch was a strike they waved their arms.

Some of them threw cushions onto the field.
After the fifth inning a fight broke out in the upper deck.
The lights went on behind third base.
The Policia rushed in with long nightsticks with lead end
It was over before the teams changed positions.

During the seventh inning someone shot the pitcher.
He was warming-up, winding-up with his left leg in the air.
He stopped for a moment, standing on one leg.
Then he laid his glove and the ball on the ground.
He sat down on the rubber with his head between his legs.

There was a lot of blood.
But after that no one cared about the game.
After the game several small black boys got on the bus.
They tried to sell their mothers and sisters to the ballplayers.
But they were not very amusing.

"My mother she es virgin," they would say.
"Pussy, she have good pussy.
Only five dolla."
The next day the pitcher was back at the hotel.
But no one came out to the pool.

Nobody went around the sky-blue bay.
Nobody wanted to see the ancient Castillo Del Morro.
Nobody cared about the long chutes down to the water.
The chutes were used to feed slaves to the sharks.
After all, that was a hundred years before.

Visiting Firenze

It has all gone too quickly, now,
my younger son, a pathologist,
the taller and thinner of the three of us,
walking point along the narrow
Via della Pergola on our daily mission
to the Uffizi or Accademia Gallery,
the Cappelle Medicee.
He pauses at the corner to look back
at me consulting my map,
attempting to navigate the maze.
Occasionally I offer a hand and/or
arm signal to stay the course,
to plod onward, or maybe to turn,
the elder son, several steps behind,
counseling vigilance, thinking
of personal injuries that might result
from speeding motorcycles
that threaten our passage,
assessing the damage, and
what the settlement for us
might be in this strange land.

So we wear away our days,
the too short time each morning
trooping out from the Residenza il Villino,
resolute, as if something spectacular
might come of it, in the Piazza Santa Croce
with pigeons, staring up at an absent Dante,
Michelangelo and Galileo firmly ensconced
in ornate casks inside, grieved by

disconsolate muses. Later we will be
mesmerized by the David
and the Allegories, the chiseling and
polishing meant to represent flesh
in stone into myth.
With sensory overload seeping in,
it is an easy mistake to make.

But even that goes quickly,
for me and these minor Medicees,
these pups, their positions, too, set,
futures assured as if anything might be
assured by grace and gifts,
preparing to become patrons,
as if we turn corners most days and
years, well-guided, but misdirected,
in to and then out of the Renaissance.

In the end we settle
at the tombs of tyrants
humbled before the mind and hand
that fashioned Dawn, Day, Dusk, Night
reclining, giving ourselves away,
willingly, as we promised to do
in the alchemy of art, medicine or law,
as we are required to,
as if each new direction,
each street is a world
to move us toward a final static
enterprise of things superbly conceived
and executed, though not quite divine.

Hesitations

Made immobile by stone visions,
in the short time we have
we hope to see what else there is,
though not without the soft regret
that turns the artist's, the physician's,
the law maker's hand
of moments to a fine dust.

The Spirit in the Machine

The day was too clear for thunder
maybe a sonic boom or dynamite
at the mine rattling windows
then prehistoric molds of recent tire tracks
crossing the yard
and stacked against a giant maple
an ancient truck hissing
like a horned serpent
that might have followed him

in a faded blue shirt baggy pants
bow-legged and bent
his white and matted hair glistening
in the bright rainbow sun
old Fayett
waved his beaten pith helmet

cooling the adaro and himself
sixty years after Guadalcanal
a tree-to-tree advance
in knee-deep infested lagoons
each tree a sanctuary
one morning on patrol or excursion
hunter and hunted parasite and host
call it what you will
watched and waiting or waited
in the jungle light of fetid water
he paused
caught by a reflective flash-patch
of dappled sunlight

Hesitations

the brown bottle-glass surface
spread with water-spider ripples
at the base of a reed
beneath a tangled mist of vines
and steaming vegetation
humidity and heat
small undulations
in a portrait of subtle tranquility

Kamikaze insects buzzed his ears
he regarded the ululation
that papillary trembling on the water
with an exactitude of nearly perfect poise
almost nothing of motion
his M-l Garand lifted and sighted

the report mumbled in the trees
echoing back
muffled through the leaves

the violent quieting waters bubbled with blood
a shattered lens-frame on a chunk of skull and flesh
the reed wavered in the wake
then tilted but did not fall
smoke drifted on the water
the din dying in his ears
he removed his helmet and fanned himself

years afterward he drove around town
it could have been any town
about the size of an island lagoon
sometimes like an apostle
in a moment of revere

he recited what he saw that day
what he always saw after that day
as if mystified
to be telling how you can
come so close to something without seeing it
without ever seeing what is there

that afternoon his truck gone off the road
on its own across the field
into the woods
ended bent against a tree
lodged at the edge of the pond

at its side he waved his pith helmet
fanning himself and the steam
spiraling away
clearing the air
the phlegmatic humors
lifting into the leaves

The Poet

Little Master Touffit straddles his stool
in the corner, wearing a conical hat
of points and curves emblazoned
with scimitars, crescent moons, and stars,
picks his nose and mumbles to himself,
when a thin inspirational spider
comes along, probably Daddy Long Legs,
poisonous but with mandibles too small
to harm humans, and sits beside
Sir Touffit, who leaps to his feet shouting
explicatives and derivatives, such as
"The spider is father to the man,"
and "To see or not to see, that is the infectivity"
and the spider having run out of fear
shrivels down to nothing and disappears.

Returning to his stool Sir Touffit
reverts to mumbling and blinking,
when another spider comes along,
this time bulbous, juicy, shiny-black
with a red hourglass on a round belly.
But you know the rest of that story.

Three Who Speak of Love

Old women speak of love
willingly – an article of faith.
For one, "a thing to go through
with someone."
She raised eight children, lost four.
Living close to death,
it did not matter to her
that love could not be learned.

Another,
abandoned by a stricken lover,
his mind lost at sea,
held his hand for years
when he could not hold hers.
Yet, with customary consistency
she would not hear him spoken ill of;
quick to remember
that "love requires adjustments."

A third,
after decades, in her necessary way,
to her dying day, even to her children,
believing "love is what is left
when the work is done,"
referred to her husband-lover
of all those years
only as "Mr. Burke."

Yes, old women speak of love
with steady hands
settling iron-skillets on the fire.

Hesitations

Imagine the Dead Alive

Raising people from the cave,
bringing them out of the sepulcher,
even one at a time, even those
who have rested there only
a few days, is no small matter.
Infusing the old form with new life,
exciting what has always been there,
laid down in exhaustion or defeat,
takes a great deal of imagining.

Imagine the maimed and beaten
and defeated at Ypres, rising
out of the earth, or at Hiroshima,
those without skin swimming in
from the sea that salted and soothed
their burnt flesh, up the Ohta-gawa,
crawling onto the banks of the blistered city
to stand, like something out of Jason
and the Argonauts, Hydra teeth lifting
from the soil, armed, scouring
the immediate surroundings
for lost flesh, for something to shroud
their seared bones, with nothing
of their wits about them, their skulls
having been hollowed by the sea and time.

On the other hand it might be easier
to go blind to the realities
and imagine the body resurrected
in an instantaneous re-assemblage

of parts, perfectly intact, made whole
by hearsay and rumor and belief,
the unabashed fantasy in which
all of the dead, not just one or two,
could be alluded to and included.
That could be a serious matter

Existence

They must have been poets,
the macaque monkeys
who after having the shit kicked out of them
by the alpha-male world,
and having the snot slapped out of them
after that, and then confined to cages,
when given a chance
in the lab, dosed-up on cocaine.
So what's new?
Given half a chance the other half
would lie like Norman Vincent Peale.
Look at it this way.
It's not that they needed the shit they lost
to hold themselves together
or that they couldn't take criticism.
They didn't. They could.
There was no remorse in that.
But having found themselves outside
the fantasy that says
"Look at the positive side,
you are good and kind and loveable,"
well, a little juice fits into that hole, nicely.

Christmas at Bluff Grange
(Circa 1943)

At seven-thirty, right on cue, following
a jingle-bell tap-dance routine you're
prompted to center stage to join
three empty chairs left from an earlier
discussion of why farmers leave the farm.

As if to disguise its make-believe permanence
a Christmas tree of layered ornaments
sulks in one corner. By then the leavings
of the box-social have been gathered up.
This is mid-century, mid-America. There's

a war to worry about. Everything is used
until it falls apart. People are dying
everywhere. At the distant end of the room,
the nearly perfect circle paper mache moon
languishes above the door shining on

an audience waiting in rows of folding
chairs, prepared to applaud. They've heard
it all before. They expect you to do
something good. They want to marvel
at an eight-year-old remembering so much.

What they won't recall is how, when you
evoke only what you want to know, how
easily memory fails. Who is the girl that
shared the box-lunch you bid on and won?
Encouraged by donations, the suggestive

Hesitations

prodding of women in the crowd,
you proffered more for the privilege
of her company than it was worth.
She's not as pretty as Juliet or spirited as Kate.
Now she's holding hands with her boyfriend

in the third row. He is fifteen and broke,
annoyed that an eight-year-old could
(even with the prompting of mothers
and aunts) out-bid him for her favors.
Then the recitation begins. In a shirt and tie,

black trousers from an older cousin,
new oversized shoes, even at eight
the words tumble out like bubbles
over a waterfall. Years later you will
still recall the lines, forgetting, sometimes,

the reindeer names, as you have
forgotten the girl's name, and the part
about "dry leaves" and "the wild hurricane."
Thinking back, it's easy to do good.
And prepared to exit right, to make an end

no longer menaced by stage-fright,
you bow to the cold artifact of the moon
above the door and whisper, as if offering
directions to the exit to those prepared
to applaud the ending, and beyond, "... and to all..."

Winning Basketball
(Circa America - 1938)

What you need for a good basketball team
is a couple little, hook-nosed Jews out in front
to steal the ball, two Niggers under the basket,

one on each side to jump and rebound,
and a big, dumb Swede in the middle.
Sandberg said the only thing dumber
than the dumbest Pollack is a smart Swede.

So you put the Square Head in the middle,
since he won't get the ball and won't
have much to do but push people around.

Then you need a hard-headed Heine or Kraut
who always knows he is right, to tell them
what to do, and a couple Chinks or a Mick
or Frog to carry the balls and wash the suits.

Of course you can't expect them to like
each other or to do what they're told,
but after a while, if they learn to play
together, you could win a game or two.

Hesitations

Called from the bullpen in the ninth
Leroy Paige contemplates the hesitations,
enough to placate the blues, maybe
a bad woman inside, the door locked,
a man wanting in from the cold,
an old bottleneck guitar
wanting to know *Can I get you now, or*
what's the score, how many's on,
who's the hitter?
An old medley here –
tied, loaded, and DiMaggio.

Oh, hesitation stockings,
hesitation blues.
Every note a step to avoid the chalk line,
or something worse.
Looking for shadows,
Lord, Lord, and angles,
baby needs a pair of shoes.
What's the hitter looking into,
what's the sun doin'?
Just no-count hangin' round.
And what's the wind got to say,
the hesitation news,
the elements?

Like a gutbucket guitar,
maybe a woman at the bar,
standin' there saying,
Yeah, Eagle on that dolla,

sayin' everything 'cept
what she's gonna do.
"In God we trust,"
she say, Wanna a man,
but gotta seea dolla fust.

Relief's an old song.
Change the pitch,
three lines, a refrain,
across the seams two or four,
hands at the belt holdin' still,
fingers flappin' on that big glove
like waving to somebody in the third row,
flappin' like a mean woman's jaws,
a woman with big eyes smiling
at you, yeah, or at some other dude.

A fast ball outside, another in,
a couple strikes, still need a sign.
Then over the top, stretched out,
long stride, foot down, arm back,
May be old, may be dumb,
full arm speed, and a hesitation,
but got more pitches,
something real that's not there,
than Wrigley got gum.

The ball fading,
a sinking inspiration,
knee high, outside, a bit of spin,
a new song of old words,
and Satch singing,

Hesitations

the onliest way he knows,
How long I gotta wait?
Must I hesitate?
the Clipper watching, waiting,
hesitating, too long, too late,
the refrain, the call

Leroy moseying off the field,
sauntering to the dugout, laughing,
steppin' over the chalk line,
telling how it's done
to somebody, yeah, anybody
who wants to listen.

"You want hear me tell?
It's easy. Sometimes
you jus' gotta know how
to make what you got hesitate."

Pleading Guilty

He drove cross-country, day and night those days,
then lost his job at thirty-three and took to drinking
to kill time until his wife discovered a bag in the closet.

The following morning, she packed her bags and left.
Three days later she took it to the police to explain.
Discovered, finally, in what had not been suspected,

she left with her belongings then turned him in. She
wanted nothing more to do with him, again, nothing
to do with the tapes and pictures, enough, a detective

said, to make you physically ill. Six children, and all
under ten. She took the evidence in, the tapes
she found although she was unaware of what he had

been doing. And why. He gave them cigarettes, drugs
and beer – performed sex acts with them, and they
performed on him. These were home videos, children

laughing, drinking, doing dope, having sex. "How
could I have married someone like that? I can't even
look at myself in the mirror. The neighbors think

we're degenerates. What could I have done? I mean,
what would Eve have done? We had to leave town.
People think my kids are sex perverts and dope addicts."

It was enough to make a decent person physically sick.
She did not know the kids or where they came from –
maybe neighborhood, on the block, hell who knows?

Hesitations

She suspected he had picked them up in the park
or at a neighborhood convenience store. She saw
children on the street at night, and then, during

the day, on her way to work. They watched the house,
and she wondered why and what they had in mind.
On her way to work she wondered about the kids

watching the house, but never thought of something
like this. He had never been in trouble before, or so his
attorney said. He "just lost it." He, too, was a victim

of child sexual abuse. "I was taking amphetamines,"
he said. "And speed left and right." He lost it, his
attorney said, a victim, too, a childhood filled

with physical and sexual abuse. He pleaded guilty
to aggravated sexual assault and child pornography.
"His actions had a devastating effect on the victims.

Six children and sex," the prosecutor said in a somber
voice. "This will continue to haunt them. We have seen
a drop in grades, bed-wetting, nightmares, hostility.

They will never be as good as they could have been.
They are spoiled goods, damaged property. They have
seen their hopes destroyed. I have sent innocent men

to jail – but not this one. Their parents had a right to
expect their goods would be respected, their hopes
honored." There was an echo to his voice of a hundred

years in a room of polished wood and leather. He had
been in trouble before, but not in court, even as a kid.
That's when he lost it. Just to the left and right.

Amphetamines and other drugs. A hundred years
of leather and polished wood. These are the things
we've seen so far," the DA said. He cried, the children

cried, his mother cried. His wife did not appear.
"My God, man. What were you thinking? Taking
pictures." And then the court was filled with tears.

People were crying. His wife did not appear. "Haven't
you heard that pictures never lie? I could have made
a case of this. What did you intend? To sell them?

For drugs? Maybe we could have made a deal, bargain
a plea. We could have made a case if there hadn't been
intent, if you hadn't tried to trade the tapes for drugs."

"My children have visited me in jail and will continue
to visit me in prison," he said. "They carried in candy
and cigarettes and cried as reparation for their sins.

They know it wasn't me. They know it wasn't their
Daddy. The Devil got in me." He cried. "All three of them
visited me in jail." On the stand he cried again,

and spoke to his mother. "I'm sorry, Mom, I'm sorry,"
he said. "It's all right, sweetheart," she replied. "I know
you've found new life in God." He looked across the

room to his mother drying her eyes. "I'm sorry if I've
hurt you,' he said, "so sorry." His attorney said, "This is
a matter of technology. People believe what they see.

Primitive bastards. What they hear they might believe
or not. But seeing? Man, videotapes of the whole thing.
We'll not talk a jury out of this. They'll believe only

what they see. There's nothing we can say." "The Devil
got in me," he said. "My kids know it ain't me doin' these
things. They know I plan to attend a Bible college.

The Lord accepted me. He knows when he sees a sorry
man. Some other person done these things, not me.
I'll preach His Word, and the Word will set me free.

He forgave Judas, and He'll forgive me. I've found new
life in Him. Society needs to bring the Lord into our
homes and schools. We've made cesspools of filth

and sin and dived in. We need the Lord living in our
homes and schools. To give us righteousness and
save us all from sin. We dive into these pits of sin.

We've made these our choices. These are our choices.
How could a man be so far gone to do something so
evil?" He told the judge, "Consider allowing me to be

castrated. The world is full of evil leading man astray.
An order from you could set me on His sanctified way.
Then I could bear scars equal to those I inflicted

on the victims." The judge said he had read of cases
for castration as a suitable remedy for sexual offenses.
"There have been times where sex offenders were

treated so there would be no new victims. But that's
beyond the law, beyond what we have here. If you
desire, you can do that on your own. I've turned

loose too many people like you. These are my children."
The judge reminded him he'd have to serve a full
thirty years. "Seeking medical attention is up to you.

Man lives in an imperfect state. But it will have no
bearing on this court. We have failed too long to cure
this kind of thing." His lawyer objected that back-to-back

terms were illegal. There will be an appeal. "No court
is perfect, no sentence ever chiseled in stone. There's
always grounds. You'll get the scar you want. The rap

you're carrying, at thirty-three, young as you are,
they'll love you in the pen. There'll be a following,
plenty of opportunities for redemption.

On the other hand, like God, the court is seldom wrong,
And as usual, God's not got a lot to say about this."

The Apprentice

We worked in a small shop, and deep,
a darkened cavern, you might say,
the sun held just outside the single door,
both chained to a daily task.
We reworked worn and broken machines,
malfunctioning paraphernalia
left at our door, a *Metropolis* of sorts
or maybe *Modern Times.*

To everything I was apprenticed,
left to record and then imagine
what might be of value to benefit others.
Otherwise I simply aided him
by whatever means, the plethora of errands
and miniscule schemes upon instruction
to secure the proper tool, make solid
or hold an assignment of items in place
until he could secure them,
and at the end of the day,
to clean the workspace,
make it whole again.
Through tedious hours
I focused bright-light from one of the spots,
a flashlight or trouble-light,
to avoid shadows, brighten the locus
upon which his eyes were set – rather than
where my wandering visions directed
by neglect or absent mindedness might go.
The illumination of his hands
was paramount – to discern

what others need see and perceive,
the enlightenment of dedication
directed where and when needed.

Learning Trees

"Tree" Harris stood six-nine,
his little brother went six-eight.
They coached the Lincoln High School
team and looked enough alike
that sometimes people mistook
the Little Tree for the big one,
until the real Tree showed up.

In the best of Midwest lingo
everyone said, "With Tree's head
so near the basket
his team can't help but win."
His hands encompassed the globe
of a basketball – could stop it, hold it,
then send it spinning
in the precise direction
and arc of his choosing.

Tall as he was, Tree didn't bend
to the wind, to look players in the eye,
he didn't bow to the Police,
the Mayor, or Senators.

At time-outs he'd stand
peering over his players' heads,
scanning the floor,
the curves and angles,
the possibilities and chances
wrapped in the black lines.

Even so, no one ever accused him
of being uppity
or thought he was out of line.
Those who looked up to him,
who had maybe read Aristotle,
but not Augustine,
and didn't know about things like this,
speculated.

Maybe as a mere high school coach,
standing that close to the river,
Tree had been misplaced in his origins.
You had to wonder about a man like Tree,
being born tall and strong and black,
looking back at you.

Three Women in a Jacuzzi

With the authority of squatters,
in a baptismal tank,
they occupy the small Jacuzzi
at the Holiday Inn.
A litter of five, six, maybe seven
of their three- and four-year-olds
dip and bob in the roiling water
beneath, behind, and around
rolls and folds of stuffed and extended flesh.
When they sit the water rises
and spills onto the tile floor.
A foamed argument announces
the excesses of sin or maybe
an appeal to thou shalt not.

There is nothing here of the Golden Mean,
nothing sagacious, celestial, apostolic.
They are mostly childlike.

More than Graces, Fates or Furies,
they are fairy-tale and fable,
blind-mice or little-pigs.
If the body is a temple,
the priests have defected.
Hucksters and money-changers
have commandeered the pleasures
of the corporeal world.

Somewhat buoyantly they stand,
made lighter on their feet

by a bubbling certitude.
They rotate through the water.
Determined to carry the Word to the world,
they do not talk about the farmer's wife,
the wolf or Jesus or the trinity.
Today it is about what they will eat.
One says, "I'm starving." The others
concur that it is that time.
They speak of what they will feed their progeny,
the flesh and blood, the future as past,
focused on proselytizing
a mundane repast of pizzas, Big Mac's
and thick-burgers from Hardees.

When the churning waters are stilled,
nearly intractable in their weighted
theology of breeding and feeding,
they pull themselves up the steps,
one at a time, an insufficient
stretch of polyester and lycra
to cover and contain
ravenous appetites and convictions.

What is Left Undone

What is it we have left undone?
The slash of sunlight on the counter-top
needs tending to. The wind willows
at the window wanting to be heard.
Yesterday he blustered like a bully.
No one listened. We were secure
in our thoughts. We still are today.

But what is there to do?
What to give away, or hoard.
Not to murder or create,
though murder may insinuate
a myth, a life of magnitude
etched in marble and mud.

Creation, on the other hand of God,
is fatal and deformed.
A finely twisted fabric
knotted at the throat of a beloved,
a golden braid of links
on a Rembrandt painting
to remind us of what we have done –
and of what there is to do, as yet,
what we have not done.

Taking the Fifth to Poetry

No longer arranged in rows,
they are now collected in clusters
at miniature tables,
instructive archipelagoes
scattered over a room still too small
for the imagination –
unless you think of them in bits
and pieces of immediate perception.

But they are all there:
the wide-eyed, as always, scheming,
plotting a good grade, buried in the disparate
contradictions of free verse, the illogic
of pleasant dreams – and those,
heads down, nodding off,

not to be undone by a head-count
of syllables and strange slant rhymes,
easing through the hum-drum,
preparing for the real world.

No one knows how long this will go on,
when we might end their travail,
this minor imprisonment
in place and time and words.

We Shall Never Part

Your sudden going numbs my saddened heart,
lifting your pliant fingers from my skin,
though I know well that we shall never part.

I know lovers seldom make a new start,
but repeat the sorry worlds they live in.
Your sudden going numbs my saddened heart.

Of course, time may find us further apart.
Most would advise that our chances are thin,
though I know well that we shall never part.

If my love for you were a work of art
I could easily sketch the small parts in.
Your sudden going numbs my saddened heart.

Truthfully, I do not know love or art,
what colors to use, or how to begin,
though I know well that we shall never part.

Canvas and stone readily accept new art;
my love for you what it has always been.
Your sudden going numbs my saddened heart,
though I know well that we shall never part.

Be a Capitalist

Do not be a capitalist too much or too little.
Yes, be as little of a capitalist as you can be.
Save your money, and be generous not only
with those who have nothing or little
though they too are capitalists, but
with the middling wastrel class,
who feed off the generosity and kindness
of strangers. You will be a stranger to them
if you offer anything but arrogance
and encouragement to take advantage
of their sadness, their misappropriation,
their capitalism of the soul, so to speak.
    So be kind, be generous, but do not be weak.
    In your generosity, by all means do not be meek.

Hesitations

Dusting Your Hands

It's time to appreciate the closing
of the door, to push the rock back
into its slot, seal the sepulture
and walk away dusting the dust
from your hands. Leave whatever
there is of spirit still intact, lifted,
as with workmen after a job well done,
or at least completed.

In a spring of what was proposed
the bending branches
of the Acacias drop us
on this plane, moving
consciousness into the long grass,
un-abiding in possibility.
Leave well enough alone,
and commiserate with hermits
in their hermitage
the last years, maybe hours
of silent discontent.

Walk the savanna with the forgotten,
as always, and stop occasionally
to converse. They need talking to,
for they are not yet at their end,
though you are, certainly.
Weep if you have time.

So much for them. May they go on.
Meanwhile, think of this.
Now think of this. Now.

Finding a Language in the Shroud

We have all seen it on occasion
in the setting sun or the moon cresting
over the waves the sacred the divine
so hoped for that when a supernova
explodes light-years ago millions
of years away and the image one day
reaches us wrapping white-light around
our senses we turn to our nearest
companion to say this is the real thing
yes the real thing intent upon transfiguring
a refined narrative into a crude hieroglyphic
imprint of blood images staining our
    muslin memory of the sublime
    constellations lost in space and time

Who is to Say We Should Mourn

Despite psychology and
Christian admonitions
people are impossible to know
or love. Even saints require
a jigger of justice to spike
their mercy and forgiveness.
Democracy doesn't help,
but feeds the mundane,
supports the common and requires
an oversight of obvious failings –
even treachery,
in favor of diversity and freedom.
Who is to say, we are told, who
is crazy and who prophetic, who
has made the best of little and
what sycophant has taken glad-handing
advantage of the uninformed?

Often the dead wrap themselves
in a grave-blanket not to insure
pleasant dreams but to warm perfidies
and ingratiation, a black flag run up
the pole of lives miss-lived and gone silly.

Arouet thought Jesuits
".. died without mourning one another."
When asked what they taught him
Joyce is reported to have said
"To order and to judge."
So, who's to say we should mourn?

Shreve's Last Words

We spoke on Saturday night,
a phone call marked with long pauses.
He said "I only have two days.
That's what the doctor said."
Followed by a pause to consider
what he had said, I did not say
"I'm sorry." I told him
"If I could I'd stretch the days out
to forty maybe fifty years."
Though that would hardly be enough,
"We're all on the same road," I said,
"just some a little ahead of the others."
Then a long pause.

He said he wanted to get the last book together
and would I read it and mark it up with advice?
Another pause for breath, and
"Follow your own suggestions,"
he said, "make it sound good."
His words hung hesitant and distant
so I agreed to listen to his voice
for a moment to take-up his voice,
to try to see the world as he saw it
from that short space, the small sounds,
the pulse running along the thin lines
carrying the few words we had left.
"Okay," I said, "I can do that."
A silence and I said "Yes,
I will do that." He thanked me
and all was silent for a long time,
and then another pause.

Shreve at the Wall of Souls

It was an old shoe
abandoned in the driveway,
an average shoe,
a smooth heel, scuffed toe,
a sole worn through
from traipsing the earth.

Shreve nailed it to the writing-room wall –
a place of honor –
then found another. And another,
until he had a whole wall of worn soles
hung like pocket-syllables,
a sanctuary for the not-yet-condemned
to gather in the dim light.

And they were there
waiting for the hammering-in of nails,
the dry-click rhyme
of casting lots on a flat rock.

They were there
with thin, worn wings beating the air,
eager for refuge.

Slipping into the shabby retreats,
some had to hold on
to avoid falling through
the holes in the soles.

He had mostly mukluks,
loafers, a moccasins or two,

and a few odd-sized clogs,
brogues, pumps, Mary Janes, Wing Tips,
an occasional high-top sneaker,
laces torn and knotted,
frayed into a thousand loose ends.

On some the vamps were torn,
the eyelets enlarged beyond use,
the throat line scarred and wrinkled,
tongues hanging loosely,
worn to silence.

But each night when he locked the door
he could hear the sighs,
the peace of darkness
laced with an occasional whimper,
the accented wailing of fright
facing the night to come.

In the morning
the wall would breath softly –
vague exhalations,
sonorous elisions,
some few souls wheezing
in the musty air, moaning,
perhaps wracked by the disquiet
of an intrusive dream,
revisiting a lost love,
connections gone wrong or simply torn off –
the perturbations
of walking the miles of earth.

Hesitations

Some stayed for weeks,
others not as long,
but all returned again,
then again,
the compelling, uncertain memories,
recriminations
or equitable words left unsaid
that always infest the poet's head,
looking for a place to hang out,
within reach,
for years,
just beyond the conciliatory.

Hitting a Curve

You have to hit
that snake on the head.
- A baseball adage

Find a snake and put aside your fear,
all the stories you've been told about
the evil and slithering nature of things
that move in ways you have not seen
before, that you cannot anticipate.
Yes, face fear, and slithered-evil,
then put yourself at the plate
and add the possibility
that it might not be a snake at all
but some other virulent ruse
or unidentified protein
that can seriously deform
the swing of the human system,
a spin-shot from the center of a cannon
with a small arc, a bit of drop and slip.
But that's reality. That's what
you have to hit on the head.

After Dinner in the Afternoon

only nine-years-old
she plies her trade today
at an afternoon dinner
among poets and historians
makers of short lines
and dense volumes listening
to the gossip of publishing
the rigors and horrors
of getting words on paper in print

at a break
an idle moment
with enough of conversation
to obscure the true dimensions
of her interest and intentions
in matters
of nutrients for the future
she chooses carefully
this child with a Gaelic name
Naivah reminds me
that I have not eaten
my pudding and wonders if . . .

Truth Charts

To clarify not quite idle talk
facing the sea on an open beach
hoping to decide what might be best
they turn to shaping piles of sand
not exactly castles
those the sea has already worn away
but hand-shaped stacks to visualize
two rows of custody for two realms
a pair of houses two children
one parent per child a month
one row square and masculine
the soft round mounds hers

to determine who will be where
in the quieted disquiet the wind picking up
breakers turn to white-caps
the molded forms hold firmly
as if some welcome high-tide cleansing
might remedy the split and wash truth clean
to ameliorate what they had begun
in the warming sun but would not stick

the fine grains tightly pressed
to speak their separate languages
invest the disparate sand-molds with more
than they can elucidate
more than bent fingers can excavate
they wait like beachcombers
for the sea coming up the beach

Dreaming Mothers

And so we dream mothers who
left us years before they reached
our old age, issuing commands,

suggestions we still may not defy
although in doing so they are younger
by far than we will ever be.

I was her age
remembering her insistence
when I was hardly any age at all.

So why recall these time-warped
phantoms that mold our minds,
who we are and will be?

Regardless, we are left with
the spirit the time and space
of those gentle admonitions.

Wayne Lanter

October, 1962

the tapping at the dormitory door
could have been a shock-wave
or a blinding flash of light
we anticipated more than that
but found a young priest
a Jesuit possibly but maybe not
pretending to be portending services

"Are you alright?" he inquired
apologetically, "Is everything okay?"

considering the hour and neighborhood
his words did not dissolve on the air
as they should have

we had studied
in the ultimatum of the afternoon
waiting for the Grozny to crest
its bow prominent in our minds
we could read between the lines
knowing well what man pretends he will do

turning dog-eared pages
I had recently followed Charlemagne
through the Roncesvalles
the travail of The Roland's
immortalized horsemen and archers
expectantly I looked
down the hall to the far end
there was no one there

Hesitations

our classmates had gone
a weekend
maybe a holiday
set aside for great events
everyone remembers
in the lounge the blank TV
without watchers
my roommate on the phone
attempted to assuage his fiancé
he held his hand over the mouth-piece

but that was the way of it
there was nothing
only a hollow plaintiff tapping
and a small priest in black
a Roman collar
looking for assurance
that the thin arrangements
of tribes and pride
would not in a single exhalation
scorch the earth

Wayne Lanter

Spelling Lessons

Yes, I can spell the days of the week.
It's the hours that get away,
misspelled and sad in their wanting,
in their demands.
I haven't thought about months or years,
eons will take care of themselves.
A few days ago, I was rational.
But it dissolved in the summer heat,
the autumn haze. So I'll hold to spelling
the days, one by one,
each, seven, then seven.
That should do it.
In Hebrew terms a good man was 888
or three times better than perfect.
I'm still 666, something less,
spelling out one day at a time,
one time a day,
hoping for one more, then two.
Hoping for the spell another day might cast
on the rational, the hopeful.

The Paradise Club

He was a Semite, the one thing I knew
for sure. And big, maybe six-four,
a cleft-chin, a lot like Robert Mitchum,
maybe *Out of the Past*, also like Mitchum,
with the single flip of a second-finger
he could wobble a still-lit butt
to the far side of the barroom.
When it struck sparks flew.

Then he got into it with a stripper's snake.
Paradise was nearly empty that night.
It was late. Mony Mony or The Stripper
blasted from an overhead speaker.
When a girl working late passed him
on the low runway he said,
"The Lord did well for you in twenty years."
His assessment was optimistic
but to amuse herself while taking it off,
left only with a medium-sized boa
kept on ice to slow activity,
she answered and in the repartee
discovered her village in Morelos
was only a foot-path or two
from where his wife had emigrated.

Following the dance
she retrieved her garments,
the bracelets, trinkets,
snake-eye rubies and Angelite.
She stopped at his table

and as she often did,
nonchalantly
hung the serpent,
now warming to the occasion,
over the back of an empty chair.
That's when the trouble began.

They talked,
spoke of The Paradise,
easy money and not much work.
Warming to the conversation,
gaining confidence and interest,
the snake poked its nostrils
into what was clearly not its business.
It had been on ice as if for centuries.

To be certain (after all, he was Semitic)
annoyed with the intrusion,
to be certain there would not be a next time,
he took the prophet by the throat
and pummeled its head on the table
splattering the three of them
with the mythic juice of forbidden fruit,
a spume of sacrificial-sacred snake oil.
That's when the trouble began.

The Scrapbook

recalling a cold wet spring
I lift a scrapbook
from the shelf of fifty years
a pile of faded photos and newsprint
a pretty good college baseball team
an obscure collage of winning and losing
to copy to an official team roster

by now the lineup has thinned
in the anonymous action of life
stretching from home plate
into fence-less possibilities –
of twenty-two
five are dead three missing

a Marine Colonel calls
to thank me
to explain
to recite a litany
of the communist menace he faced in Nam

another proffers appreciation in a card
that announces his bereavement and grief
for a daughter he recently buried

others reply under assumed names
insurance salesmen
teachers and thieves
wagging beneath clubhouse epithets
to which they willingly answer
and intend to carry to the grave

some other few want to know
the scrapbook's origins
who kept it

no one knows what it is
in making history
that we do not understand
in the end
and then there are those
who dared not write or call

Hesitations

Che Guevara at My Door

I didn't answer.
There were too many
derelicts in the neighborhood,
too many knocks
and broken wine bottles
in the hall, the acrid stench
of piss-soaked cheap carpeting
on the stairs.

Not that I imagined they would go away
or that he might return at a better time –
I did not consider
looking down on the street,
the last street in the city,
a large graveyard across the alley
at the edge of the lake.

I didn't answer the door
and he didn't knock again.
He moved on to other parts,
other wars,
and I was left to go mano-a-mano
without the purity of cause
or devotion to impose
a bloodshed of my views
upon the cluttered streets
giving a derelict life small order
and, in that,
the impossibility of repose.

Sister Rothschild

Somewhat beneath a clouded haven
of the second floor maternity ward
a red-face laced corpulence
in the middle-parts of her fortune

Sister Rothschild's blackened-widow
habit rustles through the interminable hours
a lifetime of not-so-antiseptic halls
skirting the issues of living and dying

each day until daily suffering quiets
finally sometime around nine o'clock
the first-floor shift going off
a few of us gathered in an ante-room

beyond her reach a six-pack
a pizza smuggled in for a fete de repit
though there is more than we surmise
the thin yellow-line of tell-tale light

beneath the door betrays our presence
our inattention to apprehend
her quiet firm but simple steps
out of which she appears

to rebuke our deference for the infirm
the dying pleading humility
caught red-handed we try to cover the fare
with a winter-coat kicking empty cans

Hesitations

beneath the table and concede to her claims
while she lobbies for her share
before acceding to our offerings
a can of beer a slice or two of pepperoni

in hand she bows graciously rotund
turns in retreat her wimple-tunic tent
her tiny feet floating quietly above a floor
of tiles worn paper-thin into forgotten years

the flip-side of the delicate-ice of too much
place in one time she disappears along
the chilled ceiling of a lower-region ward
where thirty or so nuns who do not speak

as she does and will not entreat for beer
or pizza but stare hollowed-eyed bound
in themselves not knowing the nourishment
aging habits of humility and care can give

A Cat Named Miller

For the Philip Miller Memorial Reading
at the Writers' Place, Kansas City, Missouri,
April 10, 2011

Cat – a West African word for friend

When we met cities were your natural habitat.
You told me you had already lived five or six
of your lives. Going street by street,
along the soft-paw paths, one alley at a time,
you had already found your way into and out of
an urban maze of alcohol and heart attacks.

But when you asked, I told you I didn't like cities,
and you were silent for a long time.
And you should have been.
No reason to debate things
handed to us by our mothers.

I told you I thought the stuff,
the stuff you were writing was very good.
Then you asked if I liked cats.
I said that that was another of my allergies.
And you said, "If you don't know cats,
how do you expect to understand people?"
Then, I was silent.

And though today I still have my doubts about cats,
I was learning about people –
and about cities –
the kind we live in without houses or streets,
or with houses we do not recognize
and streets we struggle to navigate.

Hesitations

And when it was my turn to ask,
I wanted to know how you found your way here.
How it was you came to the Midwest –
and I don't mean by birth,
the accidents of place and time
our mothers get us into.
I wanted to know in this winter
how you came to the heartland
of willow trees, shaded brooks and soft grass –
how you made it all up out of concrete and brick.
I wanted to know who was responsible for that –
who asked you to paint petals on a black bough –
and to think about cities and cats?

You said you didn't know how it worked,
only that it seemed necessary
and that's probably where the cats came in –
through the small door left open on cold nights,
maybe a bad-weather door for them to get inside
with sleet and smoke in their fur –

all kinds of cats – big cats, old and not so old,
irascible cats, bald-headed-bad-ass cats,
and gentle ones curled up
in villanelle hair-balls on the sofa –
long, intricate, narrative-conversational
and exotic cats,
and short, tough, beady-eyed one-line cats,
many withered and worn,
but always visionary cats.

Some dragged in stories as absurd as our own.
Maybe a cool-cat in shades,
his fur set in four-bar solo corn-rows,
his head filled with a nasty harp-riff of blue-notes
you put there.
Or a Calico-German Expressionist
with black stripes that looked like a small, fuzzy zebra.

Even cats without fur,
skinned cats –
those sad,
estranged approximations of our deepest loves
and fears.

And the one outside in the weather –
a long-hair called memory
that won't come in.
He sits at the window in the wind and snow
with a pad and pencil, watching us.
They're all here.

But now I have another question.
I want to know why you left,
and what to do about the cats?
They're touchy,
wandering around looking for someone
to rub up against,
wanting to know when you'll be back.
I told them
this is the way things go in the city.
Sometimes the streets are very dark.
Sometimes the sun doesn't shine for days,

Hesitations

maybe weeks.
But they don't believe me.
They stare off into the distances,
memorizing constellations and supernovas.
Of course there's the allergy nonsense.
They think I'm trying to get rid of them.
I'm not.

Anyway, there's a room full of cats
looking for you.
So I thought I should ask.

Of course I'll take care of them
until you get here.
I mean, what else can I do?
And if not, at least for as long as I can.

Blind

George Kimball had one working eye,
as the story goes, one of glass, though
two, the day in an angry fit he threw it
at Norman Mailer to make a blunt point.
That left him with one to see what really
was there. Or as the Chinese note in the British
affectation of monocles, "They simply do not
wish to see more than they can understand."
What Mailer did with the eye, I'm not sure,
if he didn't throw it back or write about it.
He wrote about every other worthless thing
that happened to him, and to many others.
   But being half blind to life is quite alright
   for those who can double down on insight.

The Memory
of a Forensic Pathologist
For JW

Forget the two-year-old
Bloated in his car seat
On a blistered summer day

Remember the sunlight
On your baby daughter's face

Forget the boy of nine
Done in by cocaine
His mother's boy-friend gave him

Remember to add olives
And artichokes to the grocery list

Forget the scarred inner thighs
Of a young woman found
On the steps of St. John's Church

Remember the DA's sneer
When you refused to arbitrarily
Assign a cause of death

Forget the broken clavicle
Of the woman bludgeoned
To death in her basement

Wayne Lanter

Remember the politicians
Who campaigned
To do away with pathology

Forget a father's grief
When he was asked to identify
A son killed in a gang dispute

Remember the judge who chided you
For not being more precise

Forget the police who looked
Away as a man in a hold-over cell
Beat another man to death

And when asked to a neighbor's cook-out
Remember to excuse yourself
Because you can't forget
The animal ribs on the grill

Hesitations

Do not think of this . . .

Do not think of this as man's inhumanity
to man or to woman – turning
from one who claims to love you,
who holds out prospects for possibilities
you cannot envision. This is a turning
that may not be meant to harm
or belittle, and later in the day, much later,
say years later, you wonder why and why
and if you were fair. You find you have
and have not been. But people walk away
from people they love, all the time.

Intermezzo

After forty years we gather
in a streetlamp-dusk, navigating
from disparate regions vaguely

remembered passages, quieted
playgrounds, old schools, abandoned
apartments, watering holes,

a church with a name we do not recall.
The stone walls, the tower and gothic
vaulting, have an extended creed,

fitted to an ancient mold. The café
wasn't here when last we spoke.
It has a cosmopolitan menu.

It's encouraging to have choices.
So we gather among the bread
and new wine, hanging tattered

vestments on old marriages, almost
marriages, children well or ill,
careers not gone completely strange.

There are windswept stories of deceits,
embarrassments. Fortunately, many
are dead. But after a repast of fine food

and special words, it's clear that hope,
tracking us with a cautious eye,
is now more obstacle than pledge?

Hesitations

Long after the testament ends
we will be shaking our heads.
The waiters at their empty tables

wanting us out, stare into the dark.
Of course, we are not unyielding.
When the hour is late we resign

ourselves to the inevitable, promise
to meet again, somewhere somehow
to further refine our predilections.

Wayne Lanter

The Proposal

After three years she said
she still loved him
as she had the first day they met
and if that was all there ever was
she would be happy just being with him.
This wasn't in question,
this was what she offered,
this was her quid pro quo.
Friends chided her
for not insisting on more.
"You can't go on like this," they said.

Taking their own advice
several married, once, twice,
and had children.
But it didn't matter to her.
She remained content, she said,
to go on as they were.
She loved him still,
as she did when they first met.

One day without fanfare or aplomb
she announced they were to be married,
and when asked why, she said, simply,
"Because he asked me if I would."

Small Town

In cummings' "pretty how town"
the old men are everywhere,
always there,
the great and small,
as if they were born
wrinkled and wizened,
a gaunt grey race
deposited in parks,
along railroad tracks
and back roads
leading into and out of town.

In the morning,
even before the doors open,
they appear on benches
outside the saloon,
village elders, they're thin hair
lifting in the breeze.

Years ago they gave up drinking,
and pretty much everything else.
There's nothing of religion here.
Not much to believe in or see.

Usually they don't have much to say
about the weather, their lives,
the old women they are still married to
or who have died.

Wayne Lanter

They speak little about errant sons,
wayward daughters,
hands or fingers lost working
in the fields and mines.

They watch the morning traffic
crawl along main street,
a few cars migrating
from one less advantageous place
to another.
They tell jokes, stories, chuckle
(about local sexual peculiarities)
and smoke roll-your-own
(pleasure has not yet abandoned them).

But when required to reconsider
they stare into the distance,
then more directly,
their blue eyes faded with cataracts,
and converse in short sentences,
laconic phrases embracing sorrow,
misadventure, what it means to live
without recompense,
without reprieve.
They tell you how to work at it,
how to get old,
how to squeeze blood
or money out of a turnip,
but never how to rectify
what they have done to the earth.

Going to Meet the Bear

I crossed the mountains with Hannibal
coaxing elephants through stones of snow.
I'm supposed to be a tourist but the days

are short and it's the wrong time of year.
More than that we pass a worn-down
town where racks of antlers decorate

abandoned cabin doors. That's all that's left –
a spring-fed spa, a gift shop without a clerk.
The corral out back accommodates a brace

of mares we no longer want to ride.
You offer one an apple. She takes it.
She'd take anything, with or without sin.

On the far side of town the road becomes
a mountain – we go on foot from there.
It's not easy. The paths are rocky and steep.

Talking doesn't help. The list is nearly
without end. But we've been here before.
We persevere, endure. Up the trail a mile

or so we find the falls and pause to stare.
The bear stands in the cascade, large
and grey, his back against the cliff.

He has nothing to say. The blue tattoo
on your shoulder blurs into a bruise.
Strange how often hope becomes a scar.

It will never heal. The water roars.
The bear is motionless – the mist rising
from the scree shrouds our retreat

Men Who Go to the Sea

Men who go down to the sea in ships
are nothing like the potters
who stay home in small mountain villages
of Naxos and prepare tomatoes,
olives and bread for transients
who may or might not appreciate the heroism
of molding clay against the odds.

On one hand we have the adventure
of storms and waves and a tossing bark,
on the other a certitude of failure,
the breakdown of clay,
either too moist or too dry,
the crumbling of a sea of hope,
a surge of the tides of indifference.

Libby

We talked about death,
not a lot, but as they say
significantly – about how to ignore it,
let it go, don't get in the way –
then how to get even,
which brought us to a dead end.

When you died I burned a candle
for three days, not the same one,
and not from both ends.
Candles have only one end,
warm, cooling wax and no flame.

www.ingramcontent.com/pod-product-compliance
Lightning Source LLC
Chambersburg PA
CBHW051828040426
42447CB00006B/421